Contents

The Victorian age

Queen Victoria was born in 1819. In 1837, when she was only 18, her uncle King William IV died, and she became queen of Great Britain and Ireland.

In 1840 Victoria married her German cousin, Albert. They had nine children; four sons and five daughters. Albert died in 1861 and for many years after his death Victoria lived a quiet life.

Victoria was very well respected by the people, who saw her as the mother of the nation. She gave her name to the Victorian Age, which covers most of the nineteenth century.

Queen Victoria reigned for 64 years. She was known for her dignity.

Timeline

1830 An early steam engine which was used to pull a train

1837 The young Queen Victoria

1840 The first postage stamp. It cost one penny and was known as the Penny Black

1854 Florence Nightingale led a team of nurses to look after soldiers injured in the Crimean War

1864 Policemen changed their top hats for helmets

1880 Light bulbs invented by Thomas Edison were the first to be used in homes

1893 Motor cars began to be manufactured. Their top speed was limited to 4mph

1897 Sixty years a queen. Victoria at her diamond jubilee

A Victorian Mill

Brian Milton

W
FRANKLIN WATTS
LONDON • SYDNEY

© Franklin Watts 1993
This edition: 2002

Franklin Watts
96 Leonard Street
London EC2A 4XD

Franklin Watts Australia
56 O'Riordan Street
Alexandria, Sydney, NSW 2015

ISBN: 0 7496 4575 X (pbk)

Dewey Decimal Classification: 725

A CIP catalogue record for this book is
available from the British Library

Editor: Belinda Weber
Designer: Janet Watson
Photographer: Martyn Chillmaid
Consultant: Adam Daber
Picture researcher: Sarah Moule

Acknowledgements: the publishers wish to
thank the staff, children and parents of
Poundswick Junior School, Manchester and the
staff of Quarry Bank Mill Trust Ltd, Styal,
Cheshire.

Additional photographs: Billie Love: 7b, 9t,
21bl, 27tl; Hulton Deutsch: 11t, 11c, 17c, 20tr,
20b, 23tr, 23bl, 25t, 25c, 26b; Mary Evans
Picture Library: 11bc, 17br, 26t; National Trust
Photographic Library © Mike Williams: 14br;
Picturepoint 4bl, 7t, 7c, 14 bl, 21 tl; Popperfoto
6c, 17tr, 23c; Quarry Bank Mill Trust Ltd: 19b,
27c; Robert Harding Picture Library: 27bl;
Rowntree Foundation: 26c.

Printed in Malaysia

A lot can be learnt about the Victorian period by looking at everyday items. Some can be easily recognised but other things look very unusual.

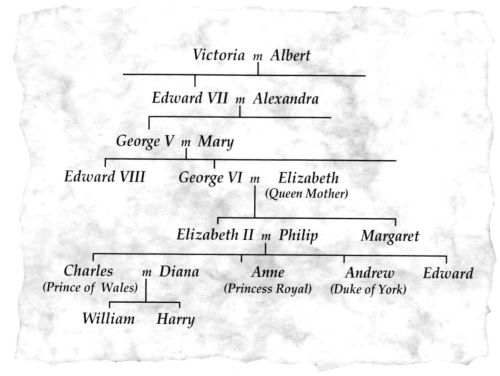

Victoria *m* Albert

Edward VII *m* Alexandra

George V *m* Mary

Edward VIII   George VI *m* Elizabeth
(Queen Mother)

Elizabeth II *m* Philip   Margaret

Charles *m* Diana   Anne   Andrew   Edward
(Prince of Wales)   (Princess Royal)   (Duke of York)

William   Harry

The British Royal Family is directly descended from Queen Victoria. Queen Elizabeth II is her great great grand daughter. The family tree does not show all Queen Victoria's relatives as she had such a large family. A number of her children were married into royal families in other countries in Europe.

The Industrial Revolution

In the years of Victoria's reign, dramatic changes took place in the way people lived. Many people moved away from the country. By the middle of the nineteenth century over half of the population lived in the towns and cities.

One of the main reasons people moved to the towns was "the enclosure movement". Acts of Parliament between 1740 and 1844 enclosed or privatised large areas of the countryside, which villagers had previously used to grow crops or graze their animals.

Machines were developed that could do the work of people. More and more goods were needed for the growing population and this changed the working life of Britain.

More and more people left the countryside to look for work in the cities and towns. The new factories dominated the skyline. This was a very different scene from the country villages they had left.

The graph shows the growth in population for Manchester during the nineteenth century. Each figure represents 10,000 people. In 1853 Manchester was granted city status and became a major British city.

Before the invention of steam engines, the only way to drive machines was to use the power of wind, water or human or animal muscle. Steam-powered machines could work anywhere at anytime, provided they had enough fuel. This meant that factories and mills could be built in cities and towns, near to where there was a ready made work force.

Railway lines were built all over Britain. The Stockton to Darlington Railway was the first to carry passengers. The Manchester to Liverpool railway was very successful. By the end of the century most parts of Britain could be reached by train.

The railway line from Manchester to Liverpool opened for passengers in 1830. The engine that pulled the train was the *Rocket* designed by George Stephenson.

? LET'S INVESTIGATE

Many changes took place during the Victorian Age. Look for the signs of change in your area. Look at buildings such as factories, mills, and schools. Do any date from this period? Find out when the railway in your area was built.

From the cottage to the factory

The making of cotton goods was one of the largest and most important industries in Britain in the nineteenth century. Before the invention of large power driven machines, cotton cloth was made in country cottages using a spinning wheel and a weaving loom. All the family shared in the work.

Families lived and worked in the same house. They worked long hours to make enough cloth to sell.

Women and girls would spin the raw cotton into thin threads called yarn.

Men and women worked on the looms. These machines turned the yarn into cloth by weaving vertical and horizontal threads together.

Whole families lived and worked in these small cottages.

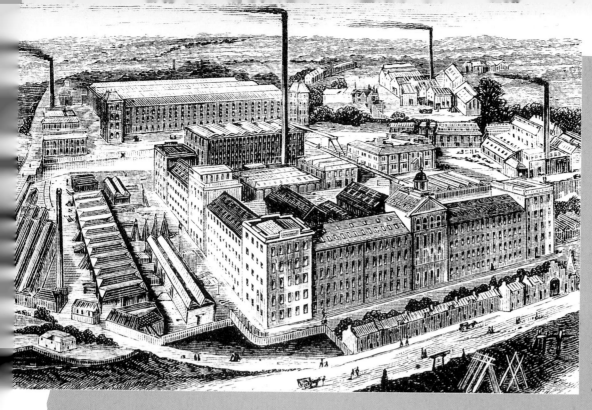

Mills and factories grew up close to each other in the expanding cities. They were often built by rivers or canals.

Factories were built to house the new machines. Where cotton was manufactured these factories were called mills. Workers moved from their cottages as most of their work was being done, much more quickly, by the machines in the factories. Small houses were built around the factory to accommodate the workers and their families. Men, women and children worked in the factories but not always in family groups. The factory system meant that people could no longer work together in their own homes.

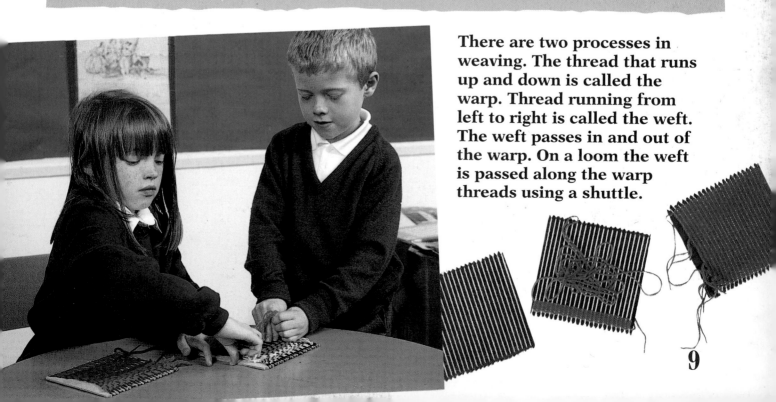

There are two processes in weaving. The thread that runs up and down is called the warp. Thread running from left to right is called the weft. The weft passes in and out of the warp. On a loom the weft is passed along the warp threads using a shuttle.

Quarry Bank Mill

Quarry Bank Mill, at Styal in the county of Cheshire, was built in 1784 by Samuel Greg. It operated as a cotton mill until 1959.

Many cotton mills were set up in the north-west of England. The main port for importing raw cotton was Liverpool.

Cotton comes from a plant which grows in hot areas. From the eighteenth century cotton was grown in the south of North America. Cotton was picked, cleaned, pressed into square bags called bales, and sent by ship to Liverpool. The cotton bales were transported to the mills by canal and road.

The mill is open to the public. People who have worked in cotton mills show how the machinery works.

Robert Greg, the son of Samuel, was in charge of the mill from 1834.

Other mills making cloth were built in towns and cities during the nineteenth century. They made cloth from wool, silk and flax, as well as cotton.

The winding room of a Lancashire Cotton Mill.

A factory making cloth near Preston, Lancashire.

Free Africans were taken by slave traders from their homes in Africa.

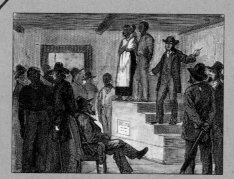

The cotton was turned into cloth in the cotton mills.

Many died on the ships that took them to America.

The cotton was baled and sent on ships to Liverpool.

They were sold as slaves and worked in the cotton fields.

For many years the manufacture of cotton cloth in Britain relied on the cotton picked by slaves.

The cotton industry

Cotton was picked by hand. The balls of cotton were picked when they were ripe.

The cotton was separated from its seed. This is called ginning. Ginned cotton was much lighter than picked cotton.

The first spinning process was to put the cotton on to a bobbin.

The warp thread was prepared for the loom by winding it on to a beam.

The cotton thread was woven into cloth on the looms.

Bleaching made the cloth as white as possible.

The bales were opened, dirt was beaten out and the cotton turned into laps, or fleecy rolls of cotton fibre.

In the carding machine, the laps were opened up, combed and passed on as slivers, or separate thin ropes.

The mule spinner spun a finer thread.

The warp thread was drawn out and a loose twist added.

Dyes were used to change the colour of the cloth.

Patterns could then be printed on to the cloth.

The mill worker

At Styal mill the people worked very long hours. In exchange they received a wage and lived in houses specially built for them in Styal village. There was a shop where the workers could buy food and other goods and what they spent was taken off their wages. The mill workers in the nearby city of Manchester earned more money than the workers at Styal, but their living conditions were not as good.

Oak Cottages at Styal were built by the Greg family and rented to the mill workers.

Workers' houses in cities were built very close together. They became known as back–to–back houses.

Old Victorian houses are still in use in many parts of the country. Over the years bathrooms and other modern facilities have been added.

Each cottage at Styal had two downstairs rooms, a cellar and two bedrooms. The cottages were occupied by a husband and wife and, often, six or seven children. The family lived in one downstairs room and used the other room for laundry. Widows, wives of mill workers who had died, lived in the cellars. People had little furniture and few possessions.

This food could have been bought in the nineteenth century. Bread and potatoes were a big part of the diet of poor people. The list shows what they would have cost in 1841 and what they cost in 1994. The wages figure is the sort of wage earned by a factory worker, like a weaver, in a full working week.

Remember that one shilling is 5p. Ten shillings is 50p and that there are 12 old pennies to the shilling and 20 shillings to a pound.

WAGES
1841 — 8 shillings (at Styal)
1994 — £250

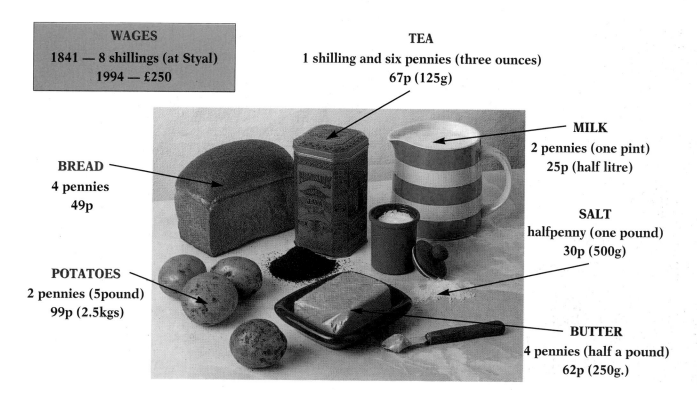

TEA
1 shilling and six pennies (three ounces)
67p (125g)

MILK
2 pennies (one pint)
25p (half litre)

BREAD
4 pennies
49p

SALT
halfpenny (one pound)
30p (500g)

POTATOES
2 pennies (5pound)
99p (2.5kgs)

BUTTER
4 pennies (half a pound)
62p (250g.)

15

Children at work

Children worked in all parts of Styal Mill. Their jobs included moving cans of fibre from the carding machine to the spinning machines and repairing broken threads. In the weaving shed they worked as "tenters". They "attended" the weaver and did whatever they were told. Their small wages helped support the whole family.

Young children joined laps together by rubbing them between their hands.

The weaving shed was a very noisy, dusty and dangerous place to work.

During the nineteenth century children worked in all sorts of factories and at other kinds of jobs. Eventually this work was limited by Acts of Parliament. Laws were introduced controlling the number of hours a day that a child could work. In 1870 the Education Act provided compulsory free full-time schooling up to the age of thirteen.

One of the great reformers was The Earl of Shaftsbury. He spent his life working to improve the lives of people, especially poor children.

Children worked down coal mines. They were sent down tunnels that could not be reached by men.

Children were used by chimney sweeps. They climbed up chimneys and swept them clean with brushes.

? LET'S INVESTIGATE

Children used to do all sorts of work. Investigate how children were used in your area. Remember to find out about domestic servants. Some authors wrote about working children. Try to find the books *Oliver Twist* by Charles Dickens and *The Water Babies* by Charles Kingsley in your local library.

The apprentice house at Styal

Children abandoned or left without parents were usually taken into orphanages. Mill and factory owners often took responsibility for these children. At Styal there is a house where the children once lived. They were called apprentices and worked at the mill for a number of years in exchange for food, lodging, clothes and a very small wage.

The apprentice house at Styal which in 1816 housed 90 children.

One of the largest rooms in the house is the kitchen.

Thomas Priestley was an apprentice at Styal in 1806."We slept in long rooms, the girls on one side of the house and the boys on the other. There were a great many beds in each room and we had clean sheets oftener than once a month, our blankets and our rugs were perfectly clean, the rooms were whitewashed once a year, and were aired every day, we had clean shirts every Sunday, and new clothes when we wanted them."

The living conditions at the house were probably better that those at the orphanage. Children were fed regularly and looked after when they were ill. They worked long hours in the mill, starting work at five-thirty in the morning and finishing at eight at night. At Styal the children were given a basic education. In the garden the apprentices grew vegetables and herbs. The house closed in 1847 when Parliament passed a law that abolished the apprentice system.

Part of these cottages was originally a Dutch Barn. Mill workers lived here.

Mill owner's children

Not all children worked in mills, up chimneys or down mines. The Greg family, who owned the mill, lived nearby in Quarry Bank House. The family lived comfortably and had servants to help with the work. The house was big and well furnished. The mill owner's children were well fed and had plenty of clothes and toys. They learned a wide range of skills, besides reading and writing, including painting and music making.

Large houses were being built on the outer areas of towns and cities. These houses provided accommodation for the family and a small number of servants.

Photography was invented in the Victorian Age. It was very expensive, and only the rich could afford to have their picture taken.

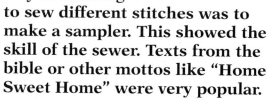

Rich children were encouraged to learn skills. Girls were taught needlework. One way of learning to sew different stitches was to make a sampler. This showed the skill of the sewer. Texts from the bible or other mottos like "Home Sweet Home" were very popular.

One of the signs of wealth was to fill the house with all sorts of furniture, ornaments and new gadgets.

Rich children were either educated at home by a tutor or governess or were sent away to private schools.

Handwriting was taught using pen and ink in a style called "copperplate"

Leisure and pastimes

People in the mill worked long hours and had little time for relaxation. Children became very good at making their own entertainment, often in the streets near their homes. They played games with simple everyday objects such as ropes and bobbins from the mill. Other toys included wooden hoops and spinning tops.

In the Victorian period richer children were able to buy a wide range of toys. Among the most popular items were dolls houses and rocking horses. Table games and jigsaws helped children with their learning.

The bobbins from the mill are being used as skittles. This is a game which has been played in different forms for many years

In this game a wooden ball is attached by a piece of string to a wooden cup. The idea is to catch the ball in the cup.

LET'S INVESTIGATE

Many of today's most famous football teams were established in the Victorian period. Find out about your local team. If you are interested in cricket look at old photographs of famous cricketers from this period. Notice the clothing and the equipment being used.

During this period many of our most famous games began to be enjoyed by all sorts of people. County and international cricket was developed and the football leagues were started. Lawn tennis was invented and The Wimbledon Championship became an annual event. Other great sporting events from this period include the boat race between Oxford and Cambridge and the development of Rugby Union and Rugby League.

More and more people began to take holidays and the seaside towns that could be reached by train were popular with richer families. Day trips were organised by churches and other groups to get workers and their families out of the cities and into countryside.

Health and education

The children who worked at Styal were luckier than most factory children. The Greg family took an interest in their workers and taught the children to read and write. When the village school was built, children from the mill were able to spend four hours a day in the school and four hours in the mill. New laws between 1870 and 1891 made going to school free and compulsory to all children up to the age of thirteen.

The school at Styal was built in 1823. It is still used by children of the village.

There was a classroom in the apprentice house. Children learnt to do their work using a slate.

At the end of the nineteenth century big schools were built in cities. All the children of the area attended these schools. Classes were large and the work was often repetitive.

Many children died in the first few years of life. Cities had very poor sanitary facilities. Sometimes whole rows of houses shared one toilet. The houses built at Styal were each provided with an outside toilet called a privy. Towards the end of the Victorian period conditions were improved in cities and towns as sewers and WCs (water closets) were built.

During the later decades of the century, the link between poor sanitation and diseases such as typhoid and cholera was recognised. Public money was spent providing sewer systems and clean water supplies to most areas of Britain.

The nineteenth century saw many improvements in the treatment of illness. At Styal, when children were ill the doctor gave them medicines based on herbs. Leeches were also used to suck "bad blood" out of people.

Religion

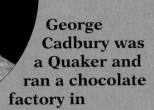

Religion played a big part in the lives of Victorian people whether rich or poor. Twice on Sunday the children from the apprentice house walked to the church at Wilmslow nearly three miles away. The first chapel was built in Styal village in 1823. Later, in 1837, another building was converted into a methodist chapel. Methodists were often feared by the mill owners as they preached about changing the factory system. However, the Greg family were happy for their workers to worship in any of the chapels or the church.

George Cadbury was a Quaker and ran a chocolate factory in Birmingham. He built a village called Bournville for his workers and did a lot of good work. He was interested in housing, adult schools and pensions for retired workers.

The Rowntree family was one of the biggest employers in the city of York. Seebohm Rowntree spent a great deal of time examining and writing about the poverty he saw in York.

Some religious organisations were established to improve the conditions of the poor. The most famous was the Salvation Army under its first leader, William Booth. His early work was with the poor in the East End of London. The Salvation Army saw itself as the army of God fighting the evils of poverty.

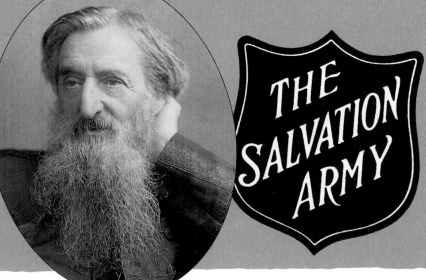

In a survey undertaken in 1851 it was found that thirty-eight per cent of all the people in the country attended church on a Sunday. Clothes were kept especially for this purpose. They were called "Sunday best".

Norcliffe Chapel Sty

On Sunday afternoons children went to church on their own. This was called going to Sunday School.

Many new churches were built in Victorian times. Most of these were built in the cities to provide religious centres for the new urban population.

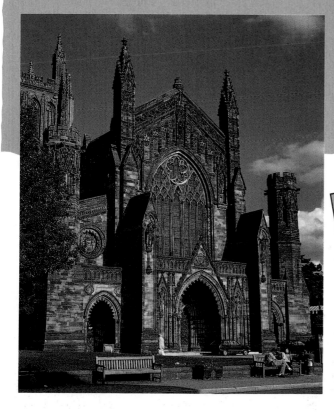

LET'S INVESTIGATE

Somewhere near you will be a church or a number of churches. Find out when they were built. If there are a number of churches find out about the different religious groups that worship there and their links with the Victorian period.

Model of the mill and village

Making a model of a mill or factory and then making workers' houses will show how the mill was much larger and how it towered over the houses. The houses in the picture are six centimetre cubes made out of cardboard. Can you work out how the row of houses was made? The factory or mill can be made out of a really large box or you could work out a way of making a large shape suitable for a factory. Try flattening out a cereal box to see how it is made.

Points to think about

- **Collect the materials you need. These could include squared paper, scissors, adhesive, ruler and pencil.**

- **Give yourself a space where you can experiment with different ideas.**

- **Make sure that the factory or mill is much bigger than the houses.**

- **Work out a method of making the roof. A triangular box will show you how to make a suitable flat shape.**

- **Think about painting your model. Look at pictures to see where the windows and doors should go.**

Machines need to be powered.
At Styal there was a fast flowing
river that could drive a
waterwheel. There was also a
steam engine which was used
when the water flow was not fast
enough to operate the machines.

More things to do

The Pre-Raphaelites

A group of Victorian artists who called themselves Pre-Raphaelites started a Back to Nature art movement. A lot of their work was based on the shapes of the natural world. They did not just paint. Artists such as William Morris used ideas for material and wall coverings, while others, such as Christina Rossetti, were writers. Patterns like the one in the picture are still popular today. They can be found in wallpaper pattern books and on curtain material.

Vegetable soup

Workers' food was very simple. This recipe for vegetable soup comes from a book called *Everyday Cookery* which was published in 1889.

RECIPE
3 onions
6 carrots
6 potatoes
4 turnips
half a pound (250 g)
of butter
four quarts (2.5 litres) of water
one head of celery
a bunch of herbs

Peel and slice the potatoes, onions, five carrots and three turnips. Fry in the butter, and pour over two quarts of boiling water. Add half the celery, a bunch of herbs, a little pepper and salt, and a crust of bread toasted very brown, and stew (simmer) for four hours. Strain through a coarse cloth or sieve. Put it into the stew pan with the remaining celery, one carrot and turnip cut prettily into shapes, and stew them tender in the soup.

Places to visit

There are many museums with collections featuring Victorian industries. These are a few of the important ones around the country. Contact your local museum for more information about your area.

- **Quarry Bank Mill,**
Styal, Cheshire, SK9 4LA

- **Armley Mills Industrial Museum,**
Canal Rd, Armley, Leeds

- **Museum of Welsh Woollen Industry,**
Dre-fach Felindre, Llandysal, Dyfed,
SA44 5UP

- **New Lanark Conservation,**
New Lanark Mills, Lanark, ML11 9DF

- **Bath Industrial Heritage Centre,**
Camden Works Museum, Julian Rd,
Bath, BA1 2RH

- **Kew Bridge Steam Museum,**
Green Dragon Lane, Brentford,
TW8 0EN

- **Ironbridge Gorge Museum,**
Telford, T58 7AW

- **The Castle Museum,**
York, YO1 1RY

- **Birmingham Museum
of Science and Industry,**
Newhall St, Birmingham, B3 1RZ

- **Manchester Museum
of Science and Industry,**
Castlefield, Manchester, M3 4JP

- **Industrial Museum,**
Courtyard Buildings, Wollaton Park,
Nottingham, NG8 2AE

- **The Black Country Museum,**
Tipton Rd, Dudley, DY1 4SQ

- **Welsh Industrial and
Maritime Museum,**
Bute St, Cardiff, CF1 6AN

- **Gladstone Pottery Museum,**
Uttoxeter Road, Longton, Stoke-on-Trent

- **Wigan Pier,**
Wigan, Lancashire

- **The Science Museum,**
Exhibition Rd, London, SW7 2DD

Index